# The Compatibility CODE

*A Practical Guide to Evaluating Compatibility Before Commitment*

## By Dr. Clover A. Perez

Clover A. Perez, LLC - New York, New York

ISBN 979-8-218-35836-5

First Edition May 2026

Published in the United States of America

Interior Typography and Cover Design by Hugh Daniel, Author's Corner

For additional copies, contact:

Dr. Clover A. Perez
https://Cloveraperez.com
Cloveraperezllc@gmail.com

For my son,
Andre K. Scott
Whose love continues to remind me that the deepest connections in life never truly leave us.

# Contents

# Acknowledgements

I would like to thank my mother, Veta J. Griffith, who has always believed in me, even during the moments when I doubt myself. Your guidance, love, and unwavering support have shaped the woman I am today, and for that, I am deeply grateful.

To my son, Dominique Jones, thank you for being one of my greatest supporters. The small moments meant more than you may realize, bringing me a bottle of water or something to eat when you saw me sitting at my desk late at night after work, still thumping away at the keyboard, trying to bring this book to life. Your acts of kindness reminded me to keep going, even on the days when I was tired.

To Treyvon, my heart, I see Andre in you every day, and that gives me strength when I feel like giving up. Your presence is a reminder that love, memory, and legacy continue to live on in the people who carry them forward.

And finally, to the person who knows exactly who they are, thank you for the many thoughtful conversations that helped inspire *The Compatibility Code*. Through our discussions about relationships, partnership, and the concept of submission, you encouraged me to think more deeply about the dynamics that shape how two people come together. Those conversations challenged me to explore these ideas with greater intention so that we could better understand one another and strive to meet on common ground.

# The Compatibility CODE

# Introduction

Relationships have always been at the heart of the human experience. They shape our identities, influence our choices, and often guide the course of our lives in ways we may not fully understand until much later.

Most people enter relationships driven by attraction, timing, or the emotional pull of connection, trusting that chemistry is a solid predictor of long-term compatibility. However, as time progresses, many realize that affection and attraction alone are inadequate to maintain a relationship that must navigate real-life challenges, pressures, and personal growth. The questions that should have been asked at the beginning of the relationship often resurface later, but by then they tend to be more complex, more painful, and significantly harder to resolve.

Compatibility cannot be assumed at the early stages of a relationship, as those stages are often exciting and emotionally intense. Instead, it requires a thoughtful and honest assessment, coupled with the willingness to look beyond mere emotions and initial attraction. This introspective journey is pivotal in determining whether two individuals possess the alignment needed to move forward and build a meaningful life together.

The purpose of *The Compatibility Code* is to bring clarity to a space often clouded by assumptions. It is designed to help individuals and couples explore the deeper aspects of compatibility that are often overlooked in the early phases of a relationship. Compatibility is not simply about enjoying the same activities or sharing similar interests. It is about alignment in values, communication patterns, emotional maturity, lifestyle expectations, and long-term vision. It is about understanding how two people respond to conflict, interpret loyalty, navigate responsibility, and define growth both individually and collectively. Without that alignment, even the most passionate connection can become strained, confusing, and unsustainable.

Many people find themselves lacking the knowledge needed to evaluate compatibility meaningfully. While they might know how to display affection or superficially sustain a relationship, they often miss the depth of understanding required to assess whether a relationship can thrive over time. Consequently, they find themselves repeating patterns, face similar challenges with different partners, or become perplexed as to why something that began with so much passion and promise fails to evolve into a lasting connection. This book offers a transformative framework that disrupts these cycles by promoting honest self-reflection, fostering direct communication, and encouraging thoughtful consideration of what truly holds significance.

*The Compatibility Code* is not meant to critique relationships, nor is it intended to sway anyone to stay or leave. Its aim is to offer a systematic, introspective, and candid approach that enables you to perceive your relationship with unprecedented clarity. By understanding where your paths converge and diverge, you can bring about a revolutionary awareness within your relationship, one that does not dismiss emotion, but rather harmonizes it, empowering you to move forward with intention rather than assumption.

The questions presented in this book go beyond simple preferences. They delve into values, beliefs, emotional responses, and life aspirations. Some questions may seem straightforward, while others might demand deeper reflection or provoke discomfort. This discomfort is not to be avoided; rather, it serves as an invitation to examine facets of oneself and one's relationships that warrant attention. Such reflection seldom arises from what is comfortable or familiar; it emerges when we are prepared to face our present realities with honesty and consider the changes that may be necessary.

At its core, the Compatibility Code encourages a deeper look at the fundamental elements that underpin relationships. It motivates individuals to go beyond simple assumptions and surface-level compatibility and examine the values, expectations, and patterns that influence the long-term health of a relationship. When approached with openness and self-awareness, this process can uncover the strengths that foster a relationship and the areas that may require more understanding, patience, or growth.

True compatibility transcends the notion of perfection. It is unrealistic to expect two individuals to connect seamlessly in every aspect. Nonetheless, there exist fundamental elements that must align sufficiently to ensure a relationship remains stable and fulfilling over time. In the absence of such cohesion, the relationship may demand ongoing adjustments, compromises that breed resentment, or emotional efforts that become exhausting. By recognizing these critical areas early, individuals can determine whether the relationship holds the promise of becoming a healthy union or requires re-evaluation before making deeper commitments.

*The Compatibility Code* is not a simple collection of questions; it is a meticulously structured journey toward insight, awareness, and decisive action. Upon completing this book, you will possess a deeper understanding of yourself, your partner, and the dynamics of your relationship. You will discern areas of congruence, areas that necessitate growth, and potential significant differences. Armed with this understanding, you will be more adept at making decisions that honor your core values, enhance your well-being, and align with your long-term vision of yourself.

As you begin this courageous journey of compatibility, embark on it with patience, grace, and honesty, giving yourself the time you need to reflect and process what you have discovered. The goal is not simply to determine whether a relationship should continue, but rather to ensure that any connection you invest in is rooted in shared values, mutual respect, emotional safety, and a unified vision for the future. With this clarity, your decisions become more deliberate, and your relationship gains stability, defined by intention rather than doubt.

It is crucial to recognize that the Compatibility Code is not meant to substitute professional, clinical, or therapeutic advice. Instead, it serves as a guided tool to foster thoughtful reflection and meaningful dialogue. Every person and relationship is imbued with its own history, complexity, and context, and no single framework can encompass every nuance. As you move through these pages, you are encouraged to engage with the material in an honest, beneficial way. Embrace the insights that resonate, explore the questions that prompt growth, and allow yourself the freedom to move past anything that does not apply to your situation.

This book is meant to assist you, not to define you. You are invited to approach the questions with openness and even a sense of enjoyment. Allow this to be an experience you share with your partner, and a meaningful way to spend quality time together while deepening your understanding of one another through honest conversation.

As you engage with the concepts within this book, allow yourself the freedom to look beyond superficial impressions and familiar narratives about love and compatibility. Reflect not only on what you hope a relationship will become but also on what it currently reveals about your values, expectations, and emotional tendencies. Though these moments of honest introspection may be challenging at times, they often lead to clarity that many relationships lack in their infancy. May the Compatibility Code encourage you to slow down, reflect thoughtfully, and approach your relationships with greater awareness and intention. Whether the insights you acquire strengthen a current relationship or prompt you to consider the path ahead, allow the lessons discovered here to steer your decisions with honesty, wisdom, and compassion.

# How To Use This Book

*The Compatibility Code* is designed to be more than a reading experience. It is a guided journey that encourages reflection, dialogue, and honest assessment. To unlock the book's full potential, one must engage deliberately, resisting the urge to rush from one section to the next.

If you choose to pursue this book individually or with a partner, this book serves as a profound instrument for introspection. If you are working through the book independently, it will serve as an aid towards a deeper understanding of your values, expectations, and emotional tendencies. In tandem with a partner, it becomes a shared experience that invites meaningful dialogue and deeper mutual understanding.

Before embarking on this journey, consider your approach. For those working with a partner, it is advisable that each person privately address the questions before engaging in discussion. This ensures each voice is articulated with clarity and authenticity, devoid of external influence or pressure.

As you move through each section, approach the questions with deliberate contemplation. While some answers may come easily, others may necessitate deeper reflection, dialogue, or even revisiting the question at a later time. There is no requirement to complete a section in one sitting. It may be beneficial to set aside dedicated time to work through a section together, free from distractions, so that each conversation can receive the attention it deserves.

Each section of the book focuses on different areas of compatibility, such as values, communication, emotional health, lifestyle, intimacy, submission, future aspirations, and personal boundaries. Upon completing the questions, you will have the opportunity to score your responses and reflect on what you have learned. The scoring system does not intend to define your relationship; rather, it offers a structured approach to identifying strengths and areas that may benefit from further conversation or development.

At the conclusion of each section, you will find guided reflection pages, a vital component of this journey. These pages invite you to capture your thoughts, chronicle conversations, and document emerging insights. Over time, such reflections will illuminate patterns and areas of both concord and divergence, thereby supporting informed decision-making.

As you engage with each section, approach the conversation with patience, attentiveness, and a sincere willingness to comprehend what is being conveyed. The purpose of these questions is not to assign blame, defend stances, or establish correctness, but rather to cultivate a deeper awareness of each person's thoughts, emotions, and responses in important areas of life. This necessitates intentional listening, posing clarifying questions when appropriate, and fostering an environment where both parties feel respected and heard. When discussions become challenging, take a pause, if necessary, return to the conversation with calm, and remain cognizant that the true value of this process lies in the mutual understanding and personal growth it fosters, rather than in prevailing in an argument or in hastening to a conclusion.

Each section of this book may offer comfort and reassurance or introduce unexplored topics within your relationship. Embrace both as crucial elements of this journey. Allow yourself permission to revisit sections, pause when necessary, and return to questions as your comprehension evolves. The aim is not to complete the book as quickly as possible, but rather to take a gradual journey that fosters insight over time. Engage with content that resonates with you, disregard what doesn't apply, and let the book's structure aid in thoughtful decision-making without constraining your ability to make choices aligned with your values and circumstances.

There will be areas where you differ in perspectives, but that doesn't mean that your relationship cannot succeed. This requires thoughtful discussion. When you encounter these differences, prioritize understanding the rationale behind each viewpoint rather than attempting to alter them prematurely. Inquire into the origins of each perspective and the experiences or beliefs shaping them. This approach nurtures deeper conversations without defensiveness or counterproductivity.

The scoring system included in the book is designed to offer structure and insight, rather than to label your relationship. The scores simply illuminate areas of differences and alignments. Use this data as a guide for further discussion rather than a conclusive assessment. The purpose of the score is to reveal patterns that might otherwise remain unnoticed, enabling you to address them with intentionality.

As you embark on this journey, ensure you create dedicated time and space so that you can stay focused and uninterrupted. Have your materials ready, approach each section with your full attention, and answer each question honestly and with care. If participating with a partner, agree on a pace that enables full, respectful participation in each discussion. The true value of this book lies in the depth of your engagement with it. Begin the first section when you are ready to embark on this transformative process.

# How The Compatibility Code Works

The questions throughout this book are not presented at random. Each section has been carefully designed to examine a specific area of compatibility that influences a relationship's long-term health. When two people first meet, attraction and chemistry often dominate the early stages of connection. While those experiences can be exciting, they rarely reveal whether two individuals truly share the values, expectations, and direction necessary to sustain a meaningful partnership over time. The purpose of this book is to move beyond surface impressions and examine the deeper elements that shape how two people relate to one another.

Each section you complete contributes to what this book calls your Compatibility Code. This code represents the combined outcome of the reflections, answers, and scores you record throughout the process. Rather than relying on assumptions or emotional impressions alone, the Compatibility Code offers a structural way to examine how well two people align across several important areas of life. These areas include personal values, communication style, emotional awareness, lifestyle expectations, intimacy, faith and belief systems, relationship roles, personal boundaries, and long-term goals.

As you progress through each section, you will notice that space is provided for scoring and reflection. These scores are not meant to reduce your relationship to numbers, nor are they intended to judge your connection. Instead, they function as a tool that helps you observe patterns that might otherwise remain unnoticed. When several areas of strong alignment appear, those results suggest that two individuals may share a similar perspective about how life and relationships should be approached. When significant differences appear, those results offer an opportunity for conversation, understanding, and thoughtful decision-making.

Towards the end of the book, you will gather the scores from each section and record them in a single place. This process will allow you to see the overall picture of your compatibility more clearly. From there, you will generate your Compatibility Code, which summarizes the level of alignment revealed through the questions you have answered together. The purpose of the code is not to declare whether a relationship should or should not continue; that is up to each person. However, it offers insight that can guide honest discussions about strengths, concerns, and expectations moving forward.

It is crucial to approach this process with great patience and a willingness to be honest with yourself and the person you're working with. Some questions may be straightforward, while others require more thought. Whatever you find that is not true for you, please discard without a second thought. The value of this process lies in honest participation, attentive listening, and a readiness to consider what the answers reveal.

When approached with openness and care, the Compatibility Code becomes more than just a set of scores; it offers a clearer picture of how two people think, what they value, and whether their vision for life and partnership truly match.

# Section One:
# Core Values

*What you believe and what matters most.*

1.  What does a meaningful life look like for you?

___________________________________________

___________________________________________

___________________________________________

2.  What are your top three values in life?

   (a)

   (b)

   (c)

3. How important is financial stability to you?

___________________________________________

___________________________________________

___________________________________________

___________________________________________

4. What does loyalty mean to you in your relationship?

_______________________________________________

_______________________________________________

_______________________________________________

5. How do you define integrity?

_______________________________________________

_______________________________________________

_______________________________________________

6. What are your long-term goals as a couple? What does commitment mean to you?

_______________________________________________

_______________________________________________

_______________________________________________

7. What is your approach to resolving conflict?

_______________________________________________

_______________________________________________

_______________________________________________

8. How important is spirituality or faith in your life?

_______________________________________________

_______________________________________________

_______________________________________________

9. Do your friends influence your life decisions? If so, how?

_______________________________________________

_______________________________________________

_______________________________________________

10. What does success look like to you?

_______________________________________________

_______________________________________________

_______________________________________________

11. Do you believe that people can change? Why or why not?

_______________________________________________

_______________________________________________

_______________________________________________

12. How do you define trust?

_______________________________________________

_______________________________________________

_______________________________________________

13. What are your non-negotiable personal values?

_______________________________________________

_______________________________________________

_______________________________________________

14. Do you believe in monogamous relationships, or do you believe in having multiple partners?

_______________________________________________

_______________________________________________

_______________________________________________

15. How do you handle feelings of jealousy or insecurity?

_______________________________________________

_______________________________________________

_______________________________________________

# Section One Score Sheet: Core Values

**Instructions: Rate your alignment for each question**

A= Strong Alignment- 4 points
B= Some Alignment- 3 points
C= Very Different- 2 points
D= Direct Conflict- 1 point

| <u>Question</u> | <u>My Score</u> | <u>Partner Score</u> | <u>Alignment</u> |
|---|---|---|---|
| 1. | _______ | _______ | _______ |
| 2. | _______ | _______ | _______ |
| 3. | _______ | _______ | _______ |
| 5. | _______ | _______ | _______ |
| 6. | _______ | _______ | _______ |
| 7. | _______ | _______ | _______ |
| 8. | _______ | _______ | _______ |
| 9. | _______ | _______ | _______ |
| 10. | _______ | _______ | _______ |
| 11. | _______ | _______ | _______ |
| 12. | _______ | _______ | _______ |
| 13. | _______ | _______ | _______ |

14. ________    ________        ________

15. ________    ________        ________

**Section Total:** ________ \ ________

<u>Circle One:</u>

**Strong Alignment \ Good Potential \ Needs Work \ Misaligned**

*Assign the numerical value for each response and record the total for this section above in the section total. Add the points from all fifteen questions to determine this section total. Once you have completed all sections in the book, add each Section Total together to determine your overall Compatibility Score, which will be used to identify your final Compatibility Code.*

# Reflection Pages

## Part 1- My Reflections

The answers that stood out most for me were...

_____________________________________

_____________________________________

_____________________________________

Something that surprised me was.........

_____________________________________

_____________________________________

_____________________________________

The areas that we are aligned in are...

_____________________________________

_____________________________________

_____________________________________

The area (s) we are not aligned in are...

_____________________________________

_____________________________________

_____________________________________

The area (s) we need growth in is...

_______________________________________________

_______________________________________________

_______________________________________________

# Part 2- Our Conversation Notes

What we agreed on...

______________________________________

______________________________________

______________________________________

What we disagreed on...

______________________________________

______________________________________

______________________________________

What needs more discussion...

______________________________________

______________________________________

______________________________________

What we learned about each other...

______________________________________

______________________________________

______________________________________

# Part 3- Looking Deeper

What this section revealed about me...

__________

__________

__________

What this section revealed about my partner...

__________

__________

__________

What I need to feel secure in this area...

__________

__________

__________

What growth is needed for us to succeed...

__________

__________

__________

# Pause and Reflect

Completing this first section is a significant endeavor deserving of recognition for the dedication and focus you have invested. Taking the time to reflect on your values and priorities, which shape your decisions, demands honesty and self-awareness. Whether you completed this section individually or collaboratively, you have embarked on an introspective journey that is often eschewed because it requires thoughtful examination and open communication. Before moving forward, allow yourself a moment to pause. Sit with what you have written, consider what resonated, and notice any insights that have begun to surface. If you are working with your partner, this may be a good time to check in with each other to reflect on newly gained understandings and ensure that you both feel ready to continue the process. Always keep in mind that there is no requirement to rush into the next section. Allocate the necessary time you both need to return with clarity and focus.

As you move into the next section, it's essential to recognize the vital role communication plays in every part of a relationship. Communication goes beyond simply speaking words during peaceful moments; it includes tone, timing, listening, body language, and the ability to respond wisely during intense emotions. Conflict isn't unavoidable in a meaningful relationship, but how you handle it can either strengthen or weaken the bond between two people. Effective communication requires being willing to listen without interrupting, to express yourself honestly without disrespect, and to handle disagreements without resorting to personal attacks.

The next section will guide you through questions that examine how you express yourself, receive feedback, and manage disagreements. How these areas are handled often determines whether a relationship becomes stronger through challenges or becomes strained. Approach the next section with the same openness and care you've shown so far, allowing the process to deepen your understanding of how you and your partner communicate during crucial moments.

# Section Two: Communication and Conflict

*How you speak, listen, disagree, and repair*

1 When you are upset, do you prefer time alone or immediate conversation?

_________________________________

_________________________________

_________________________________

2. How do you typically express frustration or anger?

_________________________________

_________________________________

_________________________________

3. When conflict arises, do you tend to speak up quickly or withdraw?

_________________________________

_________________________________

_________________________________

4. How do you usually apologize when you are wrong?

_______________________________________________

_______________________________________________

_______________________________________________

5. What does a sincere apology sound like to you?

_______________________________________________

_______________________________________________

_______________________________________________

6. Do you raise your voice during disagreements? Why or why not?

_______________________________________________

_______________________________________________

_______________________________________________

7. How do you handle criticism from your partner?

_______________________________________________

_______________________________________________

_______________________________________________

_______________________________________________

8.What makes you feel heard in a conversation?

_________________________________________________

_________________________________________________

_________________________________________________

9. How do you respond when you feel disrespected?

_________________________________________________

_________________________________________________

_________________________________________________

10. Do you bring up past issues during new arguments: Why or why not?

_________________________________________________

_________________________________________________

_________________________________________________

11. How do you repair the relationship after a disagreement?

_________________________________________________

_________________________________________________

_________________________________________________

12. What communication habits are you currently working to improve?

______________________________________________

______________________________________________

______________________________________________

13. Are you comfortable having difficult conversations about serious topics? Explain.

______________________________________________

______________________________________________

______________________________________________

14. How do you prefer to resolve conflict when emotions are high?

______________________________________________

______________________________________________

______________________________________________

15. What does respectful communication look like to you during disagreement?

______________________________________________

______________________________________________

______________________________________________

# Section Two Score Sheet- Communication and Conflict

*Instructions: Rate your alignment for each question*

A=Strong Alignment- 4 points
B-Some Alignment- 3 points
C-Very Different- 2 points
D=Direct Conflict- 1 point

| Question | My Score | Partner Score | Alignment |
| --- | --- | --- | --- |
| 1. | _______ | _______ | _______ |
| 2. | _______ | _______ | _______ |
| 3. | _______ | _______ | _______ |
| 4. | _______ | _______ | _______ |
| 5. | _______ | _______ | _______ |
| 6. | _______ | _______ | _______ |
| 7. | _______ | _______ | _______ |
| 8. | _______ | _______ | _______ |
| 9. | _______ | _______ | _______ |
| 10. | _______ | _______ | _______ |
| 11. | _______ | _______ | _______ |
| 12. | _______ | _______ | _______ |

13. ________   ________   ________

14. ________   ________   ________

15. ________   ________   ________

**Section Total:** ________/ _______

<u>Circle One:</u>

**Strong Alignment / Good Potential / Needs Work / Misaligned**

*Assign the numerical value for each response and record the total for this section above in the section total. Add the points from all fifteen questions to determine this section total. Once you have completed all sections in the book, add each Section Total together to determine your overall Compatibility Score, which will be used to identify your final Compatibility Code.*

# Reflection Pages

## Part 1- My Reflections

The answers that stood out the most to me were...

_______________________________________________

_______________________________________________

_______________________________________________

Something that surprised me was...

_______________________________________________

_______________________________________________

_______________________________________________

The areas we communicate well are...

_______________________________________________

_______________________________________________

_______________________________________________

The area (s) we need to improve on...

_______________________________________________

_______________________________________________

_______________________________________________

# Part 2- Our Conversation Notes

What we agree on...

_______________________________________________

_______________________________________________

_______________________________________________

What we disagreed on...

_______________________________________________

_______________________________________________

_______________________________________________

What needs more discussion...

_______________________________________________

_______________________________________________

_______________________________________________

What we learned about each other...

_______________________________________________

_______________________________________________

_______________________________________________

How am I feeling right now...

___________________________________________

31

___________________________________________


___________________________________________

# Part 3- Looking Deeper

What this section revealed about me...

_________________________________________________

_________________________________________________

_________________________________________________

What this section revealed about my partner...

_________________________________________________

_________________________________________________

_________________________________________________

What I need in order to feel heard and respected...

_________________________________________________

_________________________________________________

_________________________________________________

What changes or growth would strengthen our communication...

_________________________________________________

_________________________________________________

_________________________________________________

# Check In with Yourself

Before proceeding, pause and reflect on your current mindset and the impressions you have gathered thus far. You have already examined your core values and scrutinized the dynamics of communication and conflict resolution within your relationship. This endeavor demands focus, sincerity, and a readiness to evaluate both strengths and areas for growth. It is entirely normal at this juncture to experience a spectrum of emotions. You might feel encouraged by your discoveries or recognize differences necessitating deeper conversation. You may now also perceive previously unacknowledged patterns that raise concerns. These emotions are integral to an introspective evaluation. Allow yourself the grace to acknowledge your feelings without diminishing their significance.

The next section transitions the focus from external interaction to internal introspection. Emotional health and self-awareness shape how you respond under pressure, manage responsibilities, and engage with others during both peaceful and tumultuous times. Without a profound understanding of your emotional reactions and behavioral tendencies, sustaining a healthy, stable partnership becomes challenging. This section aims to facilitate an honest and accountable examination of these aspects. As you advance, approach each question with patience and lucidity, allowing the necessary time for thoughtful responses, and remain attentive to what your answers disclose about your internal patterns. When you are prepared, continue to the next section and begin your exploration of emotional health and self-awareness.

# Section Three: Emotional Health and Self-Awareness

*Understanding your internal patterns, emotional responses, and personal responsibility in a relationship*

1. How would you describe your emotional temperament during stressful situations?

_______________________________________________

_______________________________________________

_______________________________________________

2. How do you typically respond when you feel hurt or disappointed?

_______________________________________________

_______________________________________________

_______________________________________________

3. Are you comfortable expressing your emotions directly? Explain your answer.

_______________________________________________

_______________________________________________

_______________________________________________

4. How do you manage your emotions when you are upset?

________________________________________________

________________________________________________

________________________________________________

5. What triggers emotional reactions in you most often?

________________________________________________

________________________________________________

________________________________________________

6. Do you take responsibility for your actions and emotional responses? In what ways?

________________________________________________

________________________________________________

________________________________________________

7. How do you handle feelings of insecurity or jealousy?

________________________________________________

________________________________________________

________________________________________________

8. When you are wrong, how easy is it for you to acknowledge it and make corrections?

_______________________________________

_______________________________________

_______________________________________

9.How do you respond to your partner's emotional needs?

_______________________________________

_______________________________________

_______________________________________

10. What role does past experience play in how you react in your current relationship?

_______________________________________

_______________________________________

_______________________________________

11. How do you process and release negative emotions?

_______________________________________

_______________________________________

_______________________________________

12. Do you seek support when you are emotionally overwhelmed? If so, how?

_______________________________________________

_______________________________________________

_______________________________________________

13. How do you demonstrate empathy towards your partner?

_______________________________________________

_______________________________________________

_______________________________________________

14. What personal growth areas are you currently working on?

_______________________________________________

_______________________________________________

_______________________________________________

15. How do you ensure that your emotional health supports, rather than harms, your relationship?

_______________________________________________

_______________________________________________

_______________________________________________

# Section Three Score Sheet- Emotional Health and Self-Awareness

*Instructions: Rate your alignment for each question*

A=Strong Alignment- 4 points
B-Some Alignment- 3 points
C-Very Different- 2 points
D=Direct Conflict- 1 point

| Question | My Score | Partner Score | Alignment |
|---|---|---|---|
| 1. | _______ | _______ | _______ |
| 2. | _______ | _______ | _______ |
| 3. | _______ | _______ | _______ |
| 4. | _______ | _______ | _______ |
| 5. | _______ | _______ | _______ |
| 6. | _______ | _______ | _______ |
| 7. | _______ | _______ | _______ |
| 8. | _______ | _______ | _______ |
| 9. | _______ | _______ | _______ |
| 10. | _______ | _______ | _______ |
| 11. | _______ | _______ | _______ |
| 12. | _______ | _______ | _______ |
| 13. | _______ | _______ | _______ |

14. ________    ________        ________

15. ________    ________        ________

**Section total:** ________/________

<u>Circle One:</u>

**Strong Alignment / Good Potential / Needs Work / Misaligned**

*Assign the numerical value for each response and record the total for this section above in the section total. Add the points from all fifteen questions to determine this section total. Once you have completed all sections in the book, add each Section Total together to determine your overall Compatibility Score, which will be used to identify your final Compatibility Code.*

# Reflection Pages

## Part 1- My Reflections

The responses that stood out most to me were...

______________________________________________

______________________________________________

______________________________________________

Something I recognized about myself was...

______________________________________________

______________________________________________

______________________________________________

One emotional strength I bring to a relationship is...

______________________________________________

______________________________________________

______________________________________________

One area I need growth is...

______________________________________________

______________________________________________

______________________________________________

# Part 2-Our Conversation Notes

What we understood about each other...

___________________________________________________

___________________________________________________

___________________________________________________

Where we differ emotionally...

___________________________________________________

___________________________________________________

___________________________________________________

What areas that need continued conversation...

___________________________________________________

___________________________________________________

___________________________________________________

What support do we need from each other...

___________________________________________________

___________________________________________________

___________________________________________________

# Part 3- Looking Deeper

What this section revealed about my emotional patterns...

_______________________________________________

_______________________________________________

_______________________________________________

What this section revealed about my partner's emotional needs...

_______________________________________________

_______________________________________________

_______________________________________________

What do I need to feel emotionally secure...

_______________________________________________

_______________________________________________

_______________________________________________

What changes or growth will strengthen our emotional health...

_______________________________________________

_______________________________________________

_______________________________________________

# Pause and Reflect

Before proceeding, allow yourself time to evaluate your current mindset and the insights gained from this section. The undertakings you have embarked upon necessitate exploring your emotional reactions, communicative tendencies, and the extent to which you embrace accountability in your relationships. This level of introspection, though occasionally discomforting, is imperative. You may discern areas where you exhibit confidence in your emotional responses, as well as patterns that have become more pronounced and warrant attention. Additionally, you might identify previously unnamed emotions. All these insights contribute to cultivating a more precise self-awareness.

Emotional well-being directly affects the stability and quality of any relationship. Your ability to recognize and regulate your reactions, and to remain accountable for your behavior, influences how you handle everyday interactions and difficult situations. Reflect on what this section has revealed about you and, if relevant, what it has highlighted about your partner's needs and responses. Identify areas that require ongoing discussion, adjustment, or personal responsibility.

Allow yourself enough time before moving forward. You might choose to step away, review your responses again, or discuss certain questions further before proceeding. When you feel ready to go on with clarity and focus, move on to the next section.

# Section Four:
# Lifestyle and Daily Living

*How your day-to-today habits, routine, and priorities shape your life together.*

1 How do you prefer to structure your daily routine, and how important is consistency in your schedule?

_______________________________________________

_______________________________________________

_______________________________________________

2. How do you manage your time between work, rest, relationships, and personal interests?

_______________________________________________

_______________________________________________

_______________________________________________

3. What does a balanced and fulfilling daily life look like to you?

_______________________________________________

_______________________________________________

_______________________________________________

4. How do you typically handle household responsibilities and shared tasks?

_______________________________________________

_______________________________________________

_______________________________________________

5. What expectations do you have regarding cleanliness, organization, and the upkeep of your living space?

_______________________________________________

_______________________________________________

_______________________________________________

6. How do you make decisions about finances, spending, and saving in your day-to-day life?

_______________________________________________

_______________________________________________

_______________________________________________

7. What role does work or career ambition play in your life, and how does it influence your availability in a relationship?

_______________________________________________

_______________________________________________

8. How do you prefer to spend your free time and weekends?

_______________________________________________

_______________________________________________

_______________________________________________

9. What level of social interaction do you need, and how do friend-ships and extended relationships fit into your daily life?

_______________________________________________

_______________________________________________

_______________________________________________

10. How do you handle differences in energy levels, schedules, or lifestyle preferences within a relationship?

_______________________________________________

_______________________________________________

_______________________________________________

11. What are your expectations regarding health, diet, exercise, and personal care?

_______________________________________________

_______________________________________________

12.How do you respond when your partner's lifestyle habits differ significantly from your own?

_________________________________________________

_________________________________________________

_________________________________________________

13. How important is personal space and individual time to you within a shared life?

_________________________________________________

_________________________________________________

_________________________________________________

14. What non-negotiable daily or weekly habits are essential for your well-being?

_________________________________________________

_________________________________________________

_________________________________________________

15. What adjustments to your current lifestyle would strengthen your ability to maintain a stable, supportive, and cooperative day-to-day partnership?

_________________________________________________

_________________________________________________

_________________________________________________

# Section Four Score Sheet- Lifestyle and Daily Living

*Instructions: Rate your alignment for each question*

A=Strong Alignment- 4 points
B-Some Alignment- 3 points
C-Very Different- 2 points
D=Direct Conflict- 1 point

| Question | My Score | Partner Score | Alignment |
|---|---|---|---|
| 1. | _______ | _______ | _______ |
| 2. | _______ | _______ | _______ |
| 3. | _______ | _______ | _______ |
| 4. | _______ | _______ | _______ |
| 5. | _______ | _______ | _______ |
| 6. | _______ | _______ | _______ |
| 7. | _______ | _______ | _______ |
| 8. | _______ | _______ | _______ |
| 9. | _______ | _______ | _______ |
| 10. | _______ | _______ | _______ |
| 11. | _______ | _______ | _______ |
| 12. | _______ | _______ | _______ |
| 13. | _______ | _______ | _______ |

14. _________   _________        _________

15. _________   _________        _________

**Section Total:** _________/ _________

<u>Circle One</u>:

**Strong Alignment / Good Potential / Needs Work / Misaligned**

*Assign the numerical value for each response and record the total for this section above in the section total. Add the points from all fifteen questions to determine this section total. Once you have completed all sections in the book, add each Section Total together to determine your overall Compatibility Score, which will be used to identify your final Compatibility Code.*

# Reflection Pages

## Part 1- My Reflections

The habits and routines that stood out most to me were...

__________________________________________________________

__________________________________________________________

__________________________________________________________

One way my lifestyle supports a relationship is...

__________________________________________________________

__________________________________________________________

__________________________________________________________

One way my lifestyle creates tension is...

__________________________________________________________

__________________________________________________________

__________________________________________________________

One practical change I can make to improve the daily life in my relationship is...

__________________________________________________________

__________________________________________________________

__________________________________________________________

# Part 2- Our Conversation Notes

What areas are we compatible in our relationship...

_______________________________________________

_______________________________________________

_______________________________________________

What area (s) are our routines or habits differ...

_______________________________________________

_______________________________________________

_______________________________________________

What adjustments may be needed...

_______________________________________________

_______________________________________________

_______________________________________________

What are we willing to work on together...

_______________________________________________

_______________________________________________

_______________________________________________

# Part 3- Looking Deeper

What this section revealed about my priorities...

What I learned about my partner's daily needs...

What I need in order to feel balanced in our relationship...

What changes am I willing to make in my daily routines to better support the overall functioning of our relationship?

# Pause and Reflect

Before progressing to the next section, allow yourself a moment to contemplate what you have just discovered. The fabric of daily life can appear ordinary on the surface, yet it is often where the true weight of compatibility is revealed, because routines, responsibilities, expectations, and personal habits subtly shape the atmosphere of a relationship over time. What you have written here transcends a mere catalog of preferences; it is a closer look at how you function in real life, how you manage your time and responsibilities, and what you require to feel steady, safe, and supported and at peace within a shared living space. If you have completed this section with a partner, reflect on the revelations about your practical life together, noting both the comforting aspects and the areas that require greater attention, negotiation, or maturity.

Give yourself the opportunity to ponder your responses without hastening to interpret them. Consider whether certain questions exposed unspoken expectations, differences in responsibilities, or presumptions about the household's operational schedule. Small disagreements in this area can escalate if ignored—not because they are dramatic, but because their recurrence in daily life can progressively undermine respect, patience, and emotional generosity. If any of your reflections deserve a second conversation, make a note now while they remain clear, and revisit them when you and your partner are prepared to speak calmly and sincerely.

When you feel ready, proceed with purpose. The next section delves into love, intimacy, and connection, asking you to examine how affection is expressed, how bonds are sustained, and how emotional and physical needs are expressed and respected. Approach this phase with the same sincerity you have practiced thus far, acknowledging that a thriving relationship necessitates both meaningful connection and practical stability, with one complementing the other.

# Section Five:
# Love, Intimacy and Connection

*How you give and receive love, define intimacy, establish boundaries, and maintain connection within a committed relationship.*

## Part 1- Emotional Connection and Affection

1 What makes you feel emotionally connected and valued within a relationship?

_____________________________________________

_____________________________________________

_____________________________________________

2. How do you typically express love and affection toward your partner?

_____________________________________________

_____________________________________________

_____________________________________________

3. In what ways do you expect your partner to express love toward you?

______________________________________________________

______________________________________________________

______________________________________________________

4. How important is physical affection in your relationship, and what forms of affection are most meaningful to you?

______________________________________________________

______________________________________________________

______________________________________________________

5. How do you define physical intimacy beyond sexual activity?

______________________________________________________

______________________________________________________

______________________________________________________

6. What boundaries do you have regarding physical touch and closeness?

______________________________________________________

______________________________________________________

______________________________________________________

7. What are your personal beliefs and values regarding sexual intimacy within a relationship?

_________________________________________________

_________________________________________________

_________________________________________________

8. How do you determine the appropriate timing for sexual intimacy when entering a new relationship?

_________________________________________________

_________________________________________________

_________________________________________________

9. What are your expectations regarding sexual exclusivity and faithfulness?

_________________________________________________

_________________________________________________

_________________________________________________

10. What are your expectations regarding commitment and exclusivity within a romantic relationship?

_________________________________________________

_________________________________________________

_________________________________________________

11. How do you define a monogamous relationship, and is that the structure you desire? Explain your reasoning.

______________________________________________

______________________________________________

______________________________________________

12. What are your thoughts and boundaries regarding non-traditional or shared intimate experiences, such as involving additional partners?

______________________________________________

______________________________________________

______________________________________________

13. What are your beliefs about marriage, and what does it represent to you personally?

______________________________________________

______________________________________________

______________________________________________

14. What are your views on divorce, and under what circumstances do you believe it is appropriate?

______________________________________________

______________________________________________

______________________________________________

15. What level of emotional, physical, and rational commitment do you expect from a long-term partner, and what are you willing to give in return?

# Section Five Score Sheet- Love, Intimacy and Connection

*Instructions: Rate your alignment for each question*

A=Strong Alignment- 4 points
B-Some Alignment- 3 points
C-Very Different- 2 points
D=Direct Conflict- 1 point

| Question | My Score | Partner Score | Alignment |
|---|---|---|---|
| 1. | _______ | _______ | _______ |
| 2. | _______ | _______ | _______ |
| 3. | _______ | _______ | _______ |
| 4. | _______ | _______ | _______ |
| 5. | _______ | _______ | _______ |
| 6. | _______ | _______ | _______ |
| 7. | _______ | _______ | _______ |
| 8. | _______ | _______ | _______ |
| 9. | _______ | _______ | _______ |
| 10. | _______ | _______ | _______ |
| 11. | _______ | _______ | _______ |
| 12. | _______ | _______ | _______ |
| 13. | _______ | _______ | _______ |

14. ________    ________        ________

15. ________    ________        ________

**Section Total:** _______ / _______

<u>Circle One:</u>

**Strong Alignment / Good Potential / Needs Work / Misaligned**

*Assign the numerical value for each response and record the total for this section above in the section total. Add the points from all fifteen questions to determine this section total. Once you have completed all sections in the book, add each Section Total together to determine your overall Compatibility Score, which will be used to identify your final Compatibility Code.*

# Reflection Pages

## Part 1- My Reflections

The responses that stood out most to me were...

_______________________________________________

_______________________________________________

_______________________________________________

One thing I learned about how I give and receive love is...

_______________________________________________

_______________________________________________

_______________________________________________

One expectation I have that needs to be clearly communicated is...

_______________________________________________

_______________________________________________

_______________________________________________

One area where I need to grow in intimacy and connection is...

_______________________________________________

_______________________________________________

_______________________________________________

Area (s) that need further discussion...

_______________________________________________

_______________________________________________

_______________________________________________

_______________________________________________

# Part 2- Our Conversation Notes

Where we aligned in emotional and physical connection...

______________________________________________

______________________________________________

______________________________________________

This is where our expectations differ...

______________________________________________

______________________________________________

______________________________________________

These are the boundaries we need to establish or respect...

______________________________________________

______________________________________________

______________________________________________

What are we willing to work on together...

______________________________________________

______________________________________________

______________________________________________

# Part 3- Looking Deeper

What this section revealed about my needs for closeness and connection...

_______________________________________

_______________________________________

_______________________________________

What I learned about my partner's expectations for intimacy...

_______________________________________

_______________________________________

_______________________________________

This is what I need in order to feel emotionally and physically secure...

_______________________________________

_______________________________________

_______________________________________

What changes or commitments would strengthen our bond...

_______________________________________

_______________________________________

_______________________________________

# Pause and Reflect

Before proceeding, take a moment to reflect on your internal reaction to this section with clarity and calmness. The material you've just engaged with requires a level of honesty that goes beyond superficial preferences, exploring deeply personal beliefs, expectations, and boundaries. Love and intimacy are often discussed in general terms, but building a meaningful connection depends on each person's willingness to be open about their needs, what they can offer, and their non-negotiables. As you review your responses, notice any areas where your answers felt certain and grounded, as well as those where hesitations, doubts, or internal conflicts appeared.

This section may have brought up conversations that are challenging to initiate, particularly those about commitment, exclusivity, and physical connection. These topics bear significant weight as they define the level of trust, safety, and respect shared between two individuals. When expectations in these areas remain unclear or unspoken, misunderstandings can arise that are difficult to mend over time. As you sit with what has emerged, assess whether your current beliefs and expectations align with the type of relationship you aspire to build and maintain.

If you completed this section in collaboration with a partner, consider what insights you have gained about their expectations. Consider how these expectations align with your own, and identify any areas needing further discussion, clearer boundaries, or a more deliberate understanding of each other's needs. If you are working independently, use this opportunity to assess whether your responses truly reflect your current reality or an ideal that has not yet been fully expressed. At this stage, awareness and clarity are essential.

There is no rush to move forward. Give yourself plenty of time to process your reflections, revisit responses that need deeper thought, and have important conversations before proceeding.

Only advance when you have a clear, steady perspective and are ready to continue with renewed understanding and purpose.

# Section Six:
# Faith, Spirituality and Beliefs

*How your spiritual convictions, moral framework, and belief system influence your relationship, your decisions, and your shared life.*

1 What do you believe about God, a higher power, or the existence of a spiritual authority?

_______________________________________________

_______________________________________________

_______________________________________________

2. How would you describe your current spiritual or religious beliefs?

_______________________________________________

_______________________________________________

_______________________________________________

3. How have your beliefs been shaped by your upbringing, experiences, or personal study?

_______________________________________________

_______________________________________________

_______________________________________________

4. How important is faith or spirituality in your daily life and decision making?

_______________________________________________

_______________________________________________

_______________________________________________

5. What spiritual practices, if any, do you observe on a regular ba-
sis?

_______________________________________________

_______________________________________________

_______________________________________________

6. What role does prayer, meditation, or reflection play in your
life?

_______________________________________________

_______________________________________________

_______________________________________________

7. What role should a religious or spiritual community play in your
life?

_______________________________________________

_______________________________________________

_______________________________________________

8. How do your beliefs influence your moral decisions and personal conduct?

____________________________________________________

____________________________________________________

____________________________________________________

9. How do you respond to people who hold beliefs different from your own?

____________________________________________________

____________________________________________________

____________________________________________________

10. How important is it that your partner shares your faith or belief system?

____________________________________________________

____________________________________________________

____________________________________________________

11. How would you handle significant differences in religious or spiritual beliefs within a relationship?

____________________________________________________

____________________________________________________

____________________________________________________

12. What boundaries would you establish to protect your beliefs within a relationship?

____________________________________________

____________________________________________

____________________________________________

13. What beliefs or values would you want to pass on to your children or future generations?

____________________________________________

____________________________________________

____________________________________________

14. How should spiritual or religious practices be incorporated into family life?

____________________________________________

____________________________________________

____________________________________________

15. What role should faith or spirituality play in the long-term direction of your relationship?

____________________________________________

____________________________________________

____________________________________________

# Section Six Score Sheet- Faith, Spirituality and Beliefs

*Instructions: Rate your alignment for each question*

A=Strong Alignment- 4 points
B-Some Alignment- 3 points
C-Very Different- 2 points
D=Direct Conflict- 1 point

| Question | My Score | Partner Score | Alignment |
|---|---|---|---|
| 1. | _______ | _______ | _______ |
| 2. | _______ | _______ | _______ |
| 3. | _______ | _______ | _______ |
| 4. | _______ | _______ | _______ |
| 5. | _______ | _______ | _______ |
| 6. | _______ | _______ | _______ |
| 7. | _______ | _______ | _______ |
| 8. | _______ | _______ | _______ |
| 9. | _______ | _______ | _______ |
| 10. | _______ | _______ | _______ |
| 11. | _______ | _______ | _______ |
| 12. | _______ | _______ | _______ |
| 13. | _______ | _______ | _______ |

14. _______  _______  _______

15. _______  _______  _______

**Section Total:** _______/ _______

<u>Circle One:</u>

**Strong Alignment / Good Potential / Needs Work / Misaligned**

*Assign the numerical value for each response and record the total for this section above in the section total. Add the points from all fifteen questions to determine this section total. Once you have completed all sections in the book, add each Section Total together to determine your overall Compatibility Score, which will be used to identify your final Compatibility Code.*

# Reflection Pages

## Part 1- My Reflections

The beliefs that are most important to me are...

_______________________________________________

_______________________________________________

_______________________________________________

One area where I feel clear and grounded is...

_______________________________________________

_______________________________________________

_______________________________________________

An area that I need to gain greater clarity is...

_______________________________________________

_______________________________________________

_______________________________________________

One step I can take to strengthen my spiritual or moral foundation is...

_______________________________________________

_______________________________________________

_______________________________________________

# Part 2- Our Conversation Notes

This is where our beliefs differ...

_______________________________________

_______________________________________

_______________________________________

This is where our beliefs align...

_______________________________________

_______________________________________

_______________________________________

These are the areas that require further conversation.......

_______________________________________

_______________________________________

_______________________________________

These are the beliefs we are willing to respect in one another.......

_______________________________________

_______________________________________

_______________________________________

# Part 3- Looking Deeper

What this section revealed about my belief system...

_____________________________________________

_____________________________________________

_____________________________________________

What I learned about my partner's convictions.......

_____________________________________________

_____________________________________________

_____________________________________________

What I need in order to feel spiritually respected...

_____________________________________________

_____________________________________________

_____________________________________________

What shared values would strengthen our relationship...

_____________________________________________

_____________________________________________

_____________________________________________

# You're Halfway Through– Now It Gets Real

Congratulations, you have reached the halfway mark of the questions in The Compatibility Code. This is not a small accomplishment. It shows your willingness to pause, reflect, and explore parts of your life that many overlook. For some, this journey may have felt steady and manageable, while others might have faced questions that require confronting difficult thoughts, experiences, or expectations. Both experiences are valid. The most important thing is your ongoing presence and engagement with the process, even when honesty and self-examination are challenging.

Allowing someone into your personal space, thoughts, values, and expectations can be difficult. It requires a level of openness that often feels uncomfortable. It means letting someone see your thought processes, reactions, beliefs, and what you need to feel respected, safe, and secure. At the same time, it requires you to see these same areas in others, sometimes in ways that challenge your assumptions or expand your understanding. Such openness can make you feel vulnerable, but it is essential for building a relationship based on clarity instead of assumptions.

As you reflect on your journey so far, think about the deep insights you've gained about yourself. You've explored your core values, how you express needs, manage conflicts, respond emotionally, follow daily routines, and your expectations about love and intimacy, along with your beliefs and convictions. Each of these areas influences how you present yourself in a relationship. Together, they form the foundation that either strengthens or weakens a partnership over time. What you've documented here isn't just theory but a true reflection of how you live, relate, and what you expect from someone else.

If you have been working through this workbook with a partner, this moment also honors the conversations you've shared. Some discussions may have been simple, while others might have needed patience, careful listening, and a willingness to understand each other without interruption or defensiveness. Despite any differences, the ability to speak honestly and listen respectfully shows maturity and the potential for growth in a relationship. If further conversation is needed in certain areas, it is important to make space for them and ensure complete transparency for both parties.

At this point, as you move forward, you have the opportunity to evaluate your readiness for a relationship based on honesty, accountability, and mutual respect. The insights you've gained about your expectations, boundaries, and areas for growth are invaluable. The next section will guide you through discussions about roles, responsibilities, and the structure of a relationship—topics closely linked to personal beliefs, cultural expectations, and individual experiences. They require careful thought, as they significantly influence decision-making, the sharing of responsibilities, and the way respect is shown in daily interactions. As you move forward, carry the clarity you've developed in earlier sections and approach the next stage of this book with honesty and dedication.

There is no rush. Take the necessary time to process what you've learned so far, revisit any responses that need more reflection, and continue any conversations that are still developing and need ongoing discussions. Move on to the next chapter when you're ready, with a clear and focused mind.

# Section Seven:
# Roles, Submission and Partnership Dynamics

*How responsibility, leadership, cooperation, and mutual respect are defined and practiced within a relationship.*

1 How do you define the roles of each partner within a committed relationship, and what responsibilities do you believe each person should carry?

_______________________________________________

_______________________________________________

_______________________________________________

_______________________________________________

2. What does leadership look like to you in a relationship, and who do you believe should carry that responsibility in different areas of life?

_______________________________________________

_______________________________________________

_______________________________________________

_______________________________________________

3. How do you distinguish between healthy guidance and controlling behaviour within a relationship?

_______________________________________________

_______________________________________________

_______________________________________________

4. What does the concept of submission mean to you personally, and how do you believe it should be practiced in a healthy relationship?

_______________________________________________

_______________________________________________

_______________________________________________

5. In what way should submission be balanced with mutual respect, shared decision making, and personal dignity?

_______________________________________________

_______________________________________________

_______________________________________________

6. What responsibilities should accompany leadership or authority in a relationship?

_______________________________________________

_______________________________________________

_______________________________________________

7. How should major decisions be made within a relationship when both partners do not initially agree?

__________________________________

__________________________________

__________________________________

8. In what areas of life do you expect to take the lead, and what area do you expect your partner to take the lead?

__________________________________

__________________________________

__________________________________

9. How do you respond when your partner challenges your decisions or leadership?

__________________________________

__________________________________

__________________________________

10. How do you hold yourself accountable for the role you expect to carry within a relationship?

__________________________________

__________________________________

__________________________________

11. What behaviors would you consider an abuse of authority or an unhealthy use of influence?

__________________________________________________

__________________________________________________

__________________________________________________

12. How do you respond when you realize you have been unfair, dismissive, or disrespectful towards your partner?

__________________________________________________

__________________________________________________

__________________________________________________

13. What does it mean to provide protection, support, and stability within a relationship, and how should those responsibilities be shared?

__________________________________________________

__________________________________________________

__________________________________________________

14. How should a couple maintain unity while still respecting each individual's independence and voice?

__________________________________________________

__________________________________________________

__________________________________________________

15. What kind of partnership structure do you believe will allow both individuals to grow, feel respected, and remain accountable over time?

____________________________________________________________________

____________________________________________________________________

____________________________________________________________________

# Section Seven Score Sheet- Roles, Submission and Partnership Dynamics

*Instruction: Rate your alignment for each question.*

A=Strong Alignment- 4 points
B-Some Alignment- 3 points
C-Very Different- 2 points
D=Direct Conflict- 1 point

| Question | My Score | Partner Score | Alignment |
|---|---|---|---|
| 1. | | | |
| 2. | | | |
| 3. | | | |
| 4. | | | |
| 5. | | | |
| 6. | | | |
| 7. | | | |
| 8. | | | |
| 9. | | | |
| 10. | | | |
| 11. | | | |
| 12. | | | |

13. ________    ________        ________

14. ________    ________        ________

15. ________    ________        ________

**Section Total**: ___________/ _________

<u>Circle One:</u>

**Strong Alignment / Good Potential / Needs Work / Misaligned**

*Assign the numerical value for each response and record the total for this section above in the section total. Add the points from all fifteen questions to determine this section total. Once you have completed all sections in the book, add each Section Total together to determine your overall Compatibility Score, which will be used to identify your final Compatibility Code.*

# Reflection Pages

## Part 1- My Reflections

The role I see myself fulfilling in a relationship is...

_______________________________________________

_______________________________________________

_______________________________________________

One responsibility I must carry with maturity is...

_______________________________________________

_______________________________________________

_______________________________________________

This area is where I need to grow in leadership or cooperation is.........

_______________________________________________

_______________________________________________

_______________________________________________

An expectation I must communicate clearly is...

_______________________________________________

_______________________________________________

_______________________________________________

# Part 2- Our Conversation Notes

This is how we understand our roles within the relationship...

This is how we will handle decision making...

This is how we will maintain respect and accountability...

These are the areas we agree to build together...

# Part 3- Looking Deeper

This section revealed the following about my expectations for structure and leadership...

_______________________________________________

_______________________________________________

_______________________________________________

Through this process, I have gained a clearer understanding of my partner's expectations for partnership......

_______________________________________________

_______________________________________________

_______________________________________________

In order for me to feel respected and secure in my role, I require...

_______________________________________________

_______________________________________________

_______________________________________________

The commitments that would create a healthy and balanced dynamic between us are...

_______________________________________________

_______________________________________________

_______________________________________________

# Section Eight:
# Boundaries, Dealbreakers and Red Flags

*How you define your limits, protect your well-being, and recognize behaviors that can harm a relationship*

1 What personal boundaries are necessary for you to feel respected and emotionally safe in a relationship?

________________________________________________

________________________________________________

________________________________________________

2. How do you communicate your boundaries to a partner, and how do you respond when those boundaries are not respected?

________________________________________________

________________________________________________

________________________________________________

3. What boundaries do you need regarding time, privacy, communication, and personal space?

________________________________________________

________________________________________________

________________________________________________

4. What behaviors from a partner would make you feel disrespected or devalued?

_______________________________________________

_______________________________________________

_______________________________________________

5.What forms of communication or conflict behavior are unacceptable to you?

_______________________________________________

_______________________________________________

_______________________________________________

6. What patterns of behavior would cause you to question the health of your relationship?

_______________________________________________

_______________________________________________

_______________________________________________

7. What are your non-negotiable dealbreakers in a relationship?

_______________________________________________

_______________________________________________

_______________________________________________

8. How do you determine the difference between an issue that can be worked through and one that requires you to step away?

______________________________________________

______________________________________________

______________________________________________

9. What values or behaviors would immediately end your willingness to continue a relationship?

______________________________________________

______________________________________________

______________________________________________

10. What warning signs do you believe indicate a lack of emotional maturity or accountability in a partner?

______________________________________________

______________________________________________

______________________________________________

11. How do you respond when you observe patterns of dishonesty, manipulation, or inconsistency?

______________________________________________

______________________________________________

______________________________________________

12. What behaviors would you consider to be the signs of a narcissist?

________________________________________

________________________________________

________________________________________

13. How do you protect your emotional, mental, and physical well-being within a relationship?

________________________________________

________________________________________

________________________________________

14. How do you maintain your identity, self-respect, and independence while in a partnership?

________________________________________

________________________________________

________________________________________

15. What standards will you hold yourself to in order to create a relationship that is safe, respectful, and stable?

________________________________________

________________________________________

________________________________________

# Section Eight Score Sheet- Boundaries, Dealbreakers and Red Flags

*Instruction: Rate your alignment for each question.*

A=Strong Alignment- 4 points
B-Some Alignment- 3 points
C-Very Different- 2 points
D=Direct Conflict 1 point

| Question | My Score | Partner Score | Alignment |
|---|---|---|---|
| 1. | _______ | _______ | _______ |
| 2. | _______ | _______ | _______ |
| 3. | _______ | _______ | _______ |
| 4. | _______ | _______ | _______ |
| 5. | _______ | _______ | _______ |
| 6. | _______ | _______ | _______ |
| 7. | _______ | _______ | _______ |
| 8. | _______ | _______ | _______ |
| 9. | _______ | _______ | _______ |
| 10. | _______ | _______ | _______ |
| 11. | _______ | _______ | _______ |
| 12. | _______ | _______ | _______ |

13. ________   ________   ________

14. ________   ________   ________

15. ________   ________   ________

**Section Total:** __________/ ____________

<u>Circle One:</u>

**Strong Alignment / Good Potential / Needs Work / Misaligned**

*Assign the numerical value for each response and record the total for this section above in the section total. Add the points from all fifteen questions to determine this section total. Once you have completed all sections in the book, add each Section Total together to determine your overall Compatibility Score, which will be used to identify your final Compatibility Code.*

# Reflection Pages

## Part 1- My Reflections

The boundaries that are most important to me are...

_______________________________________________

_______________________________________________

_______________________________________________

The areas that I need to be more firm in protecting myself are...

_______________________________________________

_______________________________________________

_______________________________________________

The behaviours I will no longer tolerate are...

_______________________________________________

_______________________________________________

_______________________________________________

One standard I must hold myself accountable to is.......

_______________________________________________

_______________________________________________

_______________________________________________

# Part 2- Our Conversation Notes

The boundaries we agree must be respected within our relationship are...

____________________________________________________________

____________________________________________________________

____________________________________________________________

The approach we will take when concerns or violations arise is...

____________________________________________________________

____________________________________________________________

____________________________________________________________

The behaviours we both recognize as unacceptable are...

____________________________________________________________

____________________________________________________________

____________________________________________________________

Our shared commitment to maintaining a respectful and healthy
relationship includes.........

____________________________________________________________

____________________________________________________________

____________________________________________________________

# Part 3- Looking Deeper

This section clarified the limits I must maintain to protect my well-being...

_______________________________________________

_______________________________________________

_______________________________________________

This process revealed the importance of accountability on our relationship...

_______________________________________________

_______________________________________________

_______________________________________________

In order to feel safe and respected, I require...

_______________________________________________

_______________________________________________

_______________________________________________

The standards that will guide my relationship decisions moving forward are...

_______________________________________________

_______________________________________________

_______________________________________________

# Recognizing the Warning Signs

The questions you just completed require a level of honesty that many people delay until their relationship has already become complicated. Talking about boundaries, dealbreakers, and warning signs often happens only when problems arise, even though it's best to understand these early on, before the relationship deepens. By taking the time to define your limits and expectations, you create clarity for yourself and your partner. This clarity goes beyond quickly dismissing others or approaching relationships with distrust; instead, it involves recognizing what is needed to feel respected, safe, and emotionally balanced, and then offering those qualities in return.

Boundaries are not punishments for others; they are affirmations of what you consider acceptable to protect your values, emotional health, and dignity. When boundaries are clearly expressed, they promote relationships built on honesty and mutual understanding. Without these boundaries, unspoken expectations often lead to silent resentment. Many people struggle to set boundaries because they fear being seen as demanding or difficult, but, in reality, clear boundaries strengthen relationships by removing confusion and preventing misunderstandings that could damage trust over time.

Dealbreakers serve a distinct yet equally significant purpose. They delineate the threshold beyond which a relationship cannot progress in a healthy manner. Although compromise and growth are essential in any relationship, certain behaviors or conditions can erode the fundamental pillars of respect and safety. Acknowledging these boundaries does not imply an unwillingness to navigate challenges; rather, it underscores the capacity to discern between ordinary difficulties that require patience and deeper issues that compromise the very integrity of the relationship itself.

Red flags often manifest subtly before evolving into conspicuous problems. In many situations, people initially present themselves through various personas at the onset of a relationship. At first, one may seem attentive, charming, and deeply invested in the connection. Over time, however, certain behaviors may unveil patterns that warrant careful attention. For instance, you may encounter individuals exhibiting pronounced narcissistic traits, where admiration and control are prioritized over empathy and respect. Alternatively, one might experience gaslighting, a manipulative tactic where reality is repeatedly denied or distorted, causing one to question one's own judgment and perception. Additionally, some may engage in love bombing, inundating a partner with excessive attention, promises, and affection initially, only to retract such behavior once emotional dependence is established.

Recognizing these behaviors requires attentiveness and discernment, as they may not manifest immediately and are often not apparent at the outset of a relationship. Thus, it is crucial to remain observant, considering not only what a person communicates but also how their actions evolve over time.

As you review what you have written in this section, take note of the boundaries that matter most to you and the standards you have set for yourself and for the person you choose to partner with. These reflections are not intended to instill fear or impose rigid expectations but rather to empower you to make informed and deliberate choices. When a person understands their own limitations and values, they are better positioned to enter relationships with confidence and clarity.

Sustaining healthy relationships requires consistent displays of respect, accountability, and emotional awareness from both parties. It requires honest communication, taking responsibility for one's actions, and confronting challenges with a readiness to listen and grow together, rather than seeking to dominate or withdraw. When these principles are embraced and thoughtfully applied, individuals are better equipped to pursue relationships that are not only emotionally fulfilling but are also anchored in maturity, integrity, and a mutual commitment to treating one another with care and consideration.

# Section Nine:
# Future Vision, Marriage and Family

*How you imagine your future, define success, and determine whether your long-term direction aligns with that of your partner.*

1 When you think about the next ten to fifteen years of your life, what kind of future do you hope to build for yourself?

_______________________________________________

_______________________________________________

_______________________________________________

_______________________________________________

2. Do you see marriage as an important part of your future, and what does marriage represent to you personally?

_______________________________________________

_______________________________________________

_______________________________________________

_______________________________________________

3. What qualities and commitments do you believe are necessary for a marriage to succeed over time?

_______________________________________________

_______________________________________________

_______________________________________________

4. How important is legal marriage to you compared to maintaining a long-term committed partnership without marriage?

_______________________________________________

_______________________________________________

_______________________________________________

5. Do you desire to have children, and how strongly do you feel about becoming a parent?

_______________________________________________

_______________________________________________

_______________________________________________

6. If you do want to have children, how many would you like to have and what kind of upbringing would you want for them?

_______________________________________________

_______________________________________________

_______________________________________________

7. If your partner did not want children, how would that influence your decision to continue the relationship?

_______________________________________________

_______________________________________________

_______________________________________________

8. What role should extended family play in your life and in the decisions that affect your household?

_______________________________________________

_______________________________________________

_______________________________________________

9. What type of living environment do you imagine for your future, including the kind of community, city, or lifestyle you prefer?

_______________________________________________

_______________________________________________

_______________________________________________

10. What level of financial stability do you believe is necessary in order to feel secure and prepared for the future?

_______________________________________________

_______________________________________________

_______________________________________________

11. How should financial responsibilities and decision making be handled within a long-term partnership or marriage?

_______________________________________________

_______________________________________________

_______________________________________________

12. How do your career goals influence the kind of life you hope to build with a partner?

_______________________________________________

_______________________________________________

_______________________________________________

13. What shared goals would you like to accomplish together as a couple over the course of your relationship?

_______________________________________________

_______________________________________________

_______________________________________________

14. How should a couple approach major life decisions when both partners have different priorities or expectations?

_______________________________________________

_______________________________________________

_______________________________________________

15. When you imagine your life many years from now, what should a successful and fulfilling partnership look like to you?

__________________________________________________

__________________________________________________

__________________________________________________

# Section Nine Score Sheet- Future Vision Marriage and Family

*Instruction: Rate your alignment for each question.*

A=Strong Alignment- 4 points
B-Some Alignment- 3 points
C-Very Different- 2 points
D=Direct Conflict- 1 point

| Question | My Score | Partner Score | Alignment |
|---|---|---|---|
| 1. | ______ | ______ | ______ |
| 2. | ______ | ______ | ______ |
| 3. | ______ | ______ | ______ |
| 4. | ______ | ______ | ______ |
| 5. | ______ | ______ | ______ |
| 6. | ______ | ______ | ______ |
| 7. | ______ | ______ | ______ |
| 8. | ______ | ______ | ______ |
| 9. | ______ | ______ | ______ |
| 10. | ______ | ______ | ______ |
| 11. | ______ | ______ | ______ |
| 12. | ______ | ______ | ______ |
| 13. | ______ | ______ | ______ |

14. _________   _________       _________

15. _________   _________       _________

**Section Total:** ___________/ ___________

<u>Circle One</u>

**Strong Alignment / Good Potential / Needs Work / Misaligned**

*Assign the numerical value for each response and record the total for this section above in the section total. Add the points from all fifteen questions to determine this section total. Once you have completed all sections in the book, add each Section Total together to determine your overall Compatibility Score, which will be used to identify your final Compatibility Code.*

# Reflection Pages

## Part 1- My Reflections

The long-term priorities that matter most are...

_______________________________________________

_______________________________________________

_______________________________________________

The expectations I have about marriage and family life are...

_______________________________________________

_______________________________________________

_______________________________________________

The areas that require deeper thought or discussions are...

_______________________________________________

_______________________________________________

_______________________________________________

The kind of future that I hope to build with a partner includes...

_______________________________________________

_______________________________________________

_______________________________________________

# Part 2- Our Conversation Notes

These are the areas that our vision for marriage and family aligns...

___________________________________________

___________________________________________

___________________________________________

The areas where our expectations for the future differ are...

___________________________________________

___________________________________________

___________________________________________

The shared goals we both feel committed to pursuing together...

___________________________________________

___________________________________________

___________________________________________

Conversations that require further discussion and clarity are...

___________________________________________

___________________________________________

___________________________________________

# Part 3- Looking Deeper

This section clarified the future priorities that will guide my life decisions...

________________________________________________

________________________________________________

________________________________________________

A greater understanding emerged regarding my partner's vision for marriage and family...

________________________________________________

________________________________________________

________________________________________________

In order for me to feel confident about our shared future, the following must be present...

________________________________________________

________________________________________________

________________________________________________

The commitments required to build a stable and fulfilling future together include...

________________________________________________

________________________________________________

________________________________________________

# Section Ten:
# Final Reflections and Compatibility Summary

*Bringing together everything you have discovered in order to evaluate the strength, clarity, and future of your relationship.*

## Personal Clarity

1 After completing this workbook, what have you learned about yourself that you did not fully recognize before?

__________________________________

__________________________________

__________________________________

__________________________________

2. Which of your personal values and expectations feel most important to protect in a relationship?

__________________________________

__________________________________

__________________________________

3. What areas of personal growth do you recognize within yourself as necessary for building a healthy relationship?

_________________________________________________________

_________________________________________________________

_________________________________________________________

4. What qualities in your partner give you confidence in the future of the relationship?

_________________________________________________________

_________________________________________________________

_________________________________________________________

5. What differences between you and your partner require continued discussion or deeper understanding?

_________________________________________________________

_________________________________________________________

_________________________________________________________

6. Which areas of compatibility between you and your partner appear strongest after completing these exercises?

_________________________________________________________

_________________________________________________________

_________________________________________________________

7. In what areas do you and your partner share strong agreement about values, beliefs, and long-term direction?

_______________________________________________

_______________________________________________

_______________________________________________

8. Which differences between you and your partner could create challenges if they remain unsolved?

_______________________________________________

_______________________________________________

_______________________________________________

9. How willing are both of you to grow, adapt, and work through challenges together?

_______________________________________________

_______________________________________________

_______________________________________________

10. Based on everything you have explored in this workbook, how do you currently view the future of your relationship?

_______________________________________________

_______________________________________________

_______________________________________________

**11. What conversations should continue between you and your partner as you move forward?**

_______________________________________________

_______________________________________________

_______________________________________________

**12. What steps would strengthen the health and stability of your relationship from this point on?**

_______________________________________________

_______________________________________________

_______________________________________________

**13. Identify the personal commitments you are prepared to make in order to contribute to a healthy and respectful relationship?**

_______________________________________________

_______________________________________________

_______________________________________________

**14.What standards must you maintain in order to protect your well-being, your dignity, and your values moving forward?**

_______________________________________________

_______________________________________________

_______________________________________________

15. Describe the qualities and characteristics that would define a strong and fulfilling partnership for you after completing this process.

_______________________________________________

_______________________________________________

_______________________________________________

# Your Compatibility Dashboard

By the time you have arrived at this juncture in the book, you have already spent time reflecting on various aspects of your identity and your approach to relationships. You have considered your values, communication style, emotional responses to challenges, expectations for intimacy, beliefs and convictions, envisioned roles for partners, boundaries safeguarding your well-being, and your aspirations for the future. Each of these areas plays an instrumental role in determining whether two individuals are truly compatible beyond the initial thrill or attraction. Each of these sections invites you to deliberate carefully and record your scores based on the alignment of your responses with those of your partner. When viewed individually, these scores provide insights into specific areas of compatibility, while collectively they offer a comprehensive view of how well two people might function together over time.

This page serves as your Compatibility Dashboard, a synthesis of all you have discovered during this journey. Instead of looking at each section separately, the dashboard provides a holistic view of your results. This makes it easier to recognize where strong alignment exists and where differences may require further conversations or thoughtful consideration.

The purpose of the Compatibility Dashboard is to consolidate the results from each section, giving you a clearer, more comprehensive picture. The dashboard empowers you to step back and observe how these components coalesce.

By the time you have arrived at this stage of the book, you have already spent time engaging in deep reflection on numerous aspects of who you are and how you approach relationships. You have considered your values, communication style, emotional responses to challenges, expectations for intimacy, beliefs and convictions, the roles you perceive for partners, boundaries that safeguard your well-being, and your vision for the future. Each of these elements significantly influences whether two individuals are genuinely compatible beyond the initial excitement or attraction. Every section invites you to reflect deeply and document scores based on the degree of alignment with your partner's responses. Individually, these scores provide insight into specific areas of compatibility. Collectively, they offer a broader view of how effectively two people may function as partners over time.

As you review the scores recorded throughout the book, take a moment to think about the significance of these numbers. Observe where both individuals share similar scores and where discrepancies may be more pronounced. These patterns often illuminate areas where a relationship is naturally aligned and where further understanding or compromise may be necessary.

Meticulously document your scores in the provided table on the following page. If you complete the questions alongside a partner, it is imperative that both participants enter their scores so they can be compared side-by-side. Once all the scores are recorded, take the time to observe the emerging pattern. Identify areas where alignment is most pronounced, while also paying keen attention to where different perspectives may exist.

The dashboard is not intended to provide a definitive judgment about your relationship. Rather, it aims to offer a clearer perspective on how your responses interconnect across critical dimensions of compatibility. In the next section, these scores will help reveal your Compatibility Code, which will provide a deeper interpretation of what these patterns may suggest regarding the potential strengths and challenges within your relationship.

# Unlocking Your Compatibility Code

Relationships are inherently intricate and multifaceted, and sometimes difficult to describe with simple language. Two individuals may share deep affection yet encounter challenges in communication. Others might align on values and life trajectories but handle emotional circumstances in diverse ways. Because relationships contain many moving parts, it can be difficult to see how all of these elements connect.

The Compatibility Code provides a means to elucidate these complexities through a coherent sequence that mirrors the architecture of a relationship. It transcends mere impressions, emotions, or assumptions, instead offering a discernible pattern that illustrates how two people relate across multiple facets of life. Each letter in the code corresponds to a specific section of the book and reflects the alignment level of your responses.

When these letters are placed together, they form a sequence that narrates the relationship's story. Some codes reveal strong consistency, indicating that two individuals share similar perspectives across numerous aspects of life. Other codes reveal a mixture of agreement and differences, suggesting that the relationship encompasses both strengths and challenges and requires greater understanding. In certain instances, the sequence may pinpoint areas where expectations or values diverge significantly, warranting careful attention.

The Compatibility Code is not intended to reduce a relationship to a mere label or prediction; rather, it offers a structured framework to interpret insights you have already gained. By viewing these results as a code, patterns can often become more recognizable and easier to discuss.

In the pages that follow, you will convert your scores into letters using a straightforward chart. Each letter signifies a degree of alignment within a particular area of compatibility. Once the letters are assigned, these letters will be arranged to form your Compatibility Code. This sequence will serve as a snapshot of how your perspectives interconnect across the dimensions explored in this book.

It is crucial to recognize that the results of your Compatibility Code should not be seen as a definitive judgment on your relationship's future. Relationships embody complexities that surpass any system of scores or categories. In some instances, the code may reveal strong alignment across various life areas. In others, it may highlight differences that necessitate patience, deeper conversation, or a mutual willingness from both individuals to grow and to understand one another more fully.

If your results indicate areas of misalignment, it does not automatically mean that a relationship cannot succeed. Many couples face differences in perspectives, expectations, or communication styles, yet they can overcome these challenges over time, with honesty and mutual effort. In certain instances, thoughtful discussion between partners can foster greater understanding, while in others, guidance from a counselor or relationship expert can provide constructive, supportive navigation through difficulties.

Regardless of your results, the future of your relationship is ultimately shaped by your choices. The reflections you have undertaken here can serve as a framework for introspection, fostering deeper understanding and decisions that honor your values and well-being. The next step will guide you through the process of interpreting your scores and revealing your Compatibility Code.

# The Compatibility Code Conversion Chart

Throughout each section of this book, you were asked a series of questions designed to explore different dimensions of compatibility within a relationship. After completing the questions in a section, each response should be assigned its corresponding numerical value. Once the values have been assigned, add the points together to calculate the Section Total.

Each section contains fifteen questions; the highest possible score for a section is sixty points, and the lowest is fifteen points. After calculating your Section Total, refer to the Score Conversion Chart below to determine the range your score falls within. That range corresponds to a Code Letter indicating the level of compatibility in that specific area of the relationship.

Keep in mind, these letters are not meant to judge your relationship positively or negatively. Instead, they help convert your recorded results into a clear format that makes patterns easier to see and discuss.

## Score Conversion Chart

| Score Range | Code Letter | Meaning |
| --- | --- | --- |
| 51-60 | A | Strong alignment in this area of the relationship |
| 41-50 | B | Generally compatible with some differences |
| 31-40 | C | Noticeable differences that require thoughtful discussions |
| 15-30 | D | Significant incompatibility in this area |

## Example

If your responses in a section add up to 52 points, that score falls within the 51-60 range on the chart. This means the section receives a Code A, indicating Strong Alignment in that area of the relationship.

If another section totals 44 points, it falls within the 41-50 range, which corresponds to a Code Letter B, indicating the relationship is Generally Compatible with some differences in that area.

Continue this process for each section of the book. Once you have identified the letter for every section, record those letters on your Compatibility Dashboard. Together, those letters form your Compatibility Code, offering a clear overview of areas where alignment is strong and where additional conversation or reflection may be beneficial.

# Write Your Compatibility Code

Using the conversion chart from the previous page, write the letter that corresponds to the score you recorded for each section. Each letter represents the level of alignment between you and your partner in that particular area of your relationship.

When all of the letters are written in order, they will form your Compatibility Code. This sequence provides a clearer view of how your perspectives align across the different dimensions throughout this book.

Take your time as you complete this page. Once the code is written, step back and observe the pattern that emerges. Some code will reveal strong consistency across multiple areas, while others may show a mixture of alignment and difference. Both outcomes offer valuable insight and can help guide thoughtful conversations about the future of the relationship.

**Record the Letters for Each Section**

Core Values:___________

Communication and Conflict:________________

Emotional Health and Self Awareness:___________

Lifestyle and Daily Living:_______________

Love, Intimacy and Connection:___________

Faith, Spirituality and Beliefs:____________

Roles, Submission and Partnership Dynamics:__________

Boundaries, Dealbreakers and Red Flag:_____________

Future Vision, Marriage and Family:_______________

# Understanding Your Compatibility Code

Now that you have written your Compatibility Code, you may begin to discern patterns within the sequence of letters. Some codes unveil strong congruence across various sections, while others present an amalgam of similarities and differences. These patterns are not intended to dictate the outcome of a relationship but rather serve as a lens through which two people approach important areas of life together.one

Each letter within your Compatibility Code symbolizes the degree of alignment between you and your partner in a specific section of the book. Collectively, they form a comprehensive illustration of how your perspectives intertwine across multiple facets of a relationship. Some couples will find that their code reflects consistent harmony in numerous areas, while others may see a combination of alignment and differences that encourages deeper conversation and understanding.

It is beneficial to approach your code with curiosity rather than apprehension. Relationships invariably consist of individuals who contribute diverse experiences, personalities, and expectations to the partnership. The Compatibility Code merely offers a means to recognize these patterns more clearly, enabling both individuals to reflect on their discoveries and consider their aspirations for growth and mutual understanding.

## Codes with Mostly A's

A code that contains many of A's denotes a strong alignment between you and your partner across several pivotal areas of life. Couples who share such results often exhibit a harmonious approach to their values, communication, expectations, and long-term aspirations. This degree of alignment can create a robust foundation for nurturing a stable relationship, fostering personal growth, and inspiring a shared commitment to future aspirations.

## Codes with a Mixture of A's and B's

Many couples may find that their code includes a combination of A's and B's. This configuration generally signifies a substantial degree of compatibility, while accommodating differing viewpoints or methodologies. Differences within this range are often manageable when both individuals are willing to listen, engage in open dialogue, and honor each other's perspectives. These variations, in many instances, can fortify the relationship, fostering growth and a broader understanding. Through sincere reflection and hopeful commitment, these differences may serve as catalysts for personal development and mutual understanding, ultimately nurturing a more profound connection.

## Codes that Include Several C's

When a code reveals multiple C's, it may imply that significant distinctions exist between partners in various aspects of life. These differences do not inherently doom the relationship; rather, they underscore the importance of engaging in meaningful dialogue and exerting mutual effort as the relationship progresses.

Couples who observe this pattern are encouraged to take time to discuss the areas where differences appear and consider the possibilities of compromise, adjustment, or deeper understanding.

## Codes that Include a D

When D's" appears within the Compatibility Code it signifies the presence of a notable difference within one or more of the sections. While this result does not irrevocably dictate the trajectory of a relationship, it underscores the necessity of careful attention and open discussion.

When encountering D's, it is important to revisit the questions in the pertinent section (s) and engage in candid discussions with your partner. At times, the guidance of a counselor or relationship professional may prove invaluable, enabling individuals to navigate these differences constructively.

## Looking at the Code as a Whole

Every letter offers a glimpse into specific facets of compatibility; however, the code's overarching pattern yields the most profound insights. It is essential to deliberate upon what your code divulges about your relationship, discerning the areas of greatest strength and those that may require further discussion. The wisdom gained through this introspective process can serve as a compass for meaningful dialogue and informed decisions about the future of your relationship.

# Moving Forward With Clarity

Completing this book signifies more than just concluding a series of questions; it embodies the dedication and focus you have devoted to understanding yourself, your aspirations, and the individual with whom you are forging or contemplating a relationship. Many people move through relationships driven largely by emotions, attraction, or convenience, without pausing to examine the elements that shape long-term compatibility. Throughout these pages, you have adopted a distinctive approach, choosing to deliberate and scrutinize the foundations that govern interpersonal interactions.

In this journey, you have contemplated values, communication styles, emotional insight, personal boundaries, beliefs, partnership roles, and long-term objectives. Each of these areas shapes the framework of a relationship. When they are understood and openly discussed, they foster stability, trust, and mutual respect. Conversely, when left unspoken or misunderstood, they often become sources of pain, confusion, disappointment, or conflict in the future. The reflections you have written within these pages signify an endeavor to bring these critical topics into the light, enabling honest consideration and fostering a commitment to positive change.

The Compatibility Code you have generated is not intended to define your relationship or confine it within a rigid category. Rather, it reflects the patterns emerging from your responses. Certain areas may reveal a strong alignment between you and your partner, indicating a shared perspective on various aspects of life. While other areas may highlight differences warranting further attention or discussion. Neither outcome should be perceived as a definitive answer regarding your future. Relationships are shaped not solely by compatibility but by the willingness of two individuals to communicate, evolve, and respect one another's needs.

What matters most is the awareness you have gained. Understanding where you and your partner align, where you diverge, and the expectations each brings to the relationship fosters sincere dialogue. Clarity enables decisions to be made with intention rather than assumption, encouraging both individuals to evaluate whether the relationship they are cultivating reflects the partnership they genuinely desire for their lives.

For some readers, the process may affirm that their relationship is grounded in shared values and mutual understanding. For others, it might uncover areas necessitating deeper dialogue before committing further. In some cases, the insights garnered may prompt individuals to reassess whether their relationship truly aligns with their long-term aspirations. Each outcome underscores the importance of thoughtful reflection over impulsive decisions.

Relationships that endure over time seldom rest on perfect compatibility. Instead, they thrive through patience, accountability, trust, and a mutual willingness to understand one another. Respect, honesty, and consistent communication often outweigh superficial similarities. When two individuals engage with openness and maturity, even differences present opportunities for learning and growth.

As you conclude this book, bear in mind that the questions you have answered and the insights you have unearthed retain their worth beyond the final page. They have the potential to continuously inform your dialogues, influence your choices, and inspire personal introspection long after this endeavor concludes. The clarity you have attained herein serves as a beacon, illuminating the type of relationship you aspire to cultivate and the values of utmost significance to you.

The direction your relationship takes is ultimately a decision you make. The reflections within these pages offer a discerning perspective on the journey ahead. Whether this journey leads to deeper commitment, ongoing discovery, or further contemplation, the understanding you now hold empowers you to proceed with heightened confidence and deliberate intention.

As you move forward with your life, may the insights you have unearthed here remain alive in your daily interactions and decisions. Relationships are not static entities; they evolve, deepen, and sometimes reveal truths previously unseen. What matters most is that you now have a clearer understanding of the elements that contribute to alignment, respect, and shared purpose.

May the understandings you have gathered serve not as rigid conclusions but as guiding principles, enabling you to approach love, partnership, and connection with wisdom, honesty, and self-awareness. The Compatibility Code transcends mere assessment of another; it also involves an introspective journey to understand oneself, one's values, and the life one aspires to create alongside another.

Wherever your journey may lead, may you move forward with clarity, courage, and the confidence that comes from knowing your worth and honoring the standards that truly matter to you.

# About the Author

**Dr. Clover A. Perez** is the CEO of A Beautiful HEART Ministries and the CEO and Editor in Chief of *RE/CLAIMED Magazine,* a publication dedicated to stories of resilience, transformation, and justice. Through her work, she has spent years engaging with individuals and communities on issues that shape people's lives, including personal growth, accountability, relationships, and the power of self-reflection.

***The Compatibility Code: A Practical Guide to Evaluating Compatibility Before Commitment*** was inspired in part by her personal relationship and by the many conversations she has had through her work with individuals navigating life, commitment, and partnership. These experiences led her to reflect deeply on the questions people often overlook when entering relationships and the importance of understanding compatibility beyond surface-level attraction.

Drawing on both personal and real-world observations, Dr. Perez created T*he Compatibility Code* as a thoughtful guide to help individuals and couples explore the deeper dimensions of relationships, including values, communication, boundaries, beliefs, and long-term goals. Her work encourages readers to approach relationships with clarity and honesty, and to engage in meaningful conversations before making lasting commitments.

Through her leadership, writing, and editorial work, Dr. Perez continues to encourage thoughtful dialogue about personal growth, relationships, and the choices that shape lives.